HISTORY

OF THE GREAT

CHICAGO FIRE,

OCTOBER 8, 9, AND 10, 1871.

Presented by

....*Agent.*

NEW YORK:
J. H. AND C. M. GOODSELL,
156 AND 158 BROADWAY.
1871.

THE SPECTATOR PRESS, Nos. 93 & 95 Liberty St., N. Y.

INSURE IN THE

New York

UNDERWRITERS AGENCY.

.... *Agent.*

CASH ASSETS,

Three Million Dollars.

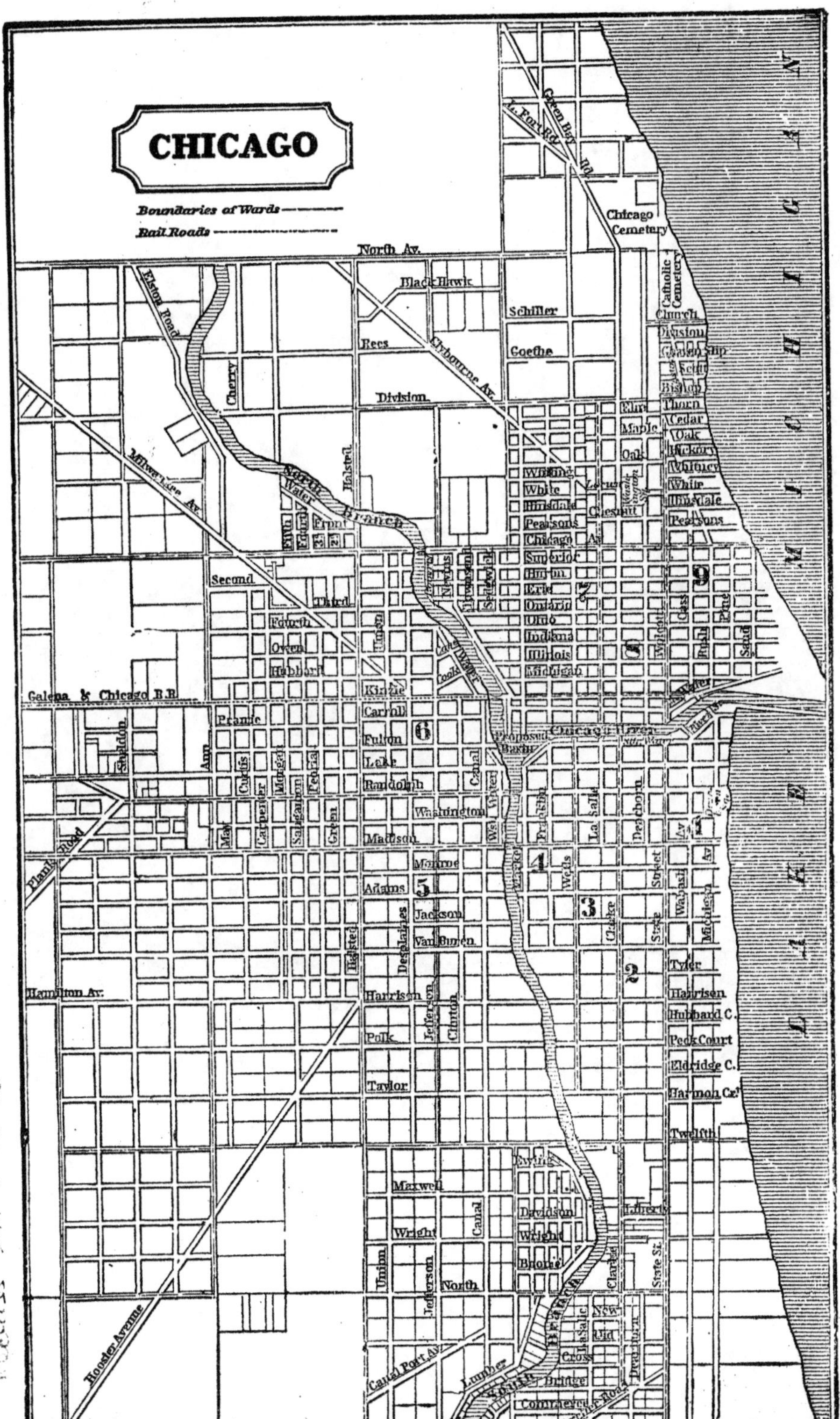
CHICAGO
Boundaries of Wards
Rail Roads
LAKE MICHIGAN
North Av.
Black Hawk
Schiller
Goethe
Rees
Clybourne Av.
Division
Cherry
Elston Road
Milwaukee Av.
Halsted
North Branch
Chicago Cemetery
Catholic Cemetery
Green Bay Rd.
Second
Third
Fourth
Owen
Hubbard
Kinzie
Carroll
Fulton
Lake
Randolph
Washington
Madison
Monroe
Adams
Jackson
Van Buren
Harrison
Polk
Taylor
Galena & Chicago R.R.
Prairie
Ann
Curtis
Carpenter
Morgan
Sangamon
Peoria
Green
Canal
Union
Jefferson
Clinton
Desplaines
Plank Road
Hamilton Av.
Hoosier Avenue
Canal Port Av.
Maxwell
Wright
North
Davidson
Boone
Lumber
Cross
Bridge
Commerce
State St.
Chicago Av.
Superior
Huron
Erie
Ontario
Ohio
Indiana
Illinois
Michigan
Church
Division
Elm
Maple
Oak
Cedar
Hickory
White
Hinsdale
Pearsons
Chestnut
Wolcott
Cass
Rush
Pine
Sand
Chicago River
Proposed Basin
Wells
La Salle
Dearborn
Clarke
State
Street
Wabash Av.
Michigan Av.
Market
Franklin
Tyler
Harrison
Hubbard C.
Peck Court
Eldridge C.
Harmon Ct.
Twelfth
Liberty
Clarke
1
2
3
4
5
6
7
8
9

THE GREAT FIRE.

A COMPREHENSIVE ACCOUNT OF THE CONFLAGRATION.

It was at 9.45 o'clock on Sunday night, October 8, when the bell sounded the alarm from box 342, for a fire which proved to be the most disastrous in the world's history. Flames were discovered in a small stable in the rear of a house on the corner of De Koven and Jefferson streets.

Hardly had the first alarm sounded when it was followed by another from the same box, and this in turn by a third, or general alarm, which summoned to that vicinity every available steam engine in the city.

The Wind

was blowing a perfect gale from the south-southwest. With terrible effect the flames leaped around in mad delight, and seized upon everything combustible. Shed after shed went down, and dwelling houses followed in rapid succession. Block after block gave way, and family after family were driven from their homes. The fire department were powerless to prevent the spreading of the calamity.

At first it was one structure on fire; then another and another were swallowed up in a whirlpool of flames, until finally it was blocks and blocks of buildings which were going down, like grass before the scythe. For upward of fifteen weeks there had been no heavy rains, and the wooden walls were dry like unto tinder in that portion of the doomed city. In vain the firemen fiercely fought the approach of the conflagration. In vain were fences and small houses hurled to the ground. In vain did the vast crowd rush hither and thither trying to save the entire west side. Onward stalked the fiery flame and red-hot air which caused all to flee from before its scorching blasts.

With the heat increased the wind, which came howling across the prairie, until at last there arose a perfect hurricane. Mighty flakes of fire, hot cinders, black, stifling smoke, were driven fiercely at the people, and amid the terrible excitement hundreds of them had their very clothes burned off their backs, as they stood there watching with tearful eyes the going down of so many houses.

When the flames had crossed over to Clinton street, between Ewing and Forquar streets, there were left probably half-a-dozen houses which

Insure with the

seemed to have been forgotten in the excitement of the moment. But they were not permitted to escape the awful flames. Backward swept the red demon, silently and softly, but swift enough to elude all pursuit, and before the terror-stricken multitude could prevent, all these frame buildings were burned to the ground.

The wind continued its roaring fierceness, and house after house was burned. To the left the fire spread forth its heat like the leaves of a fan until all of the eastern side of Jefferson street was enveloped in the furnace. To the right it had been driven with great fierceness, and Clinton street and Canal street and Beach street, and then the railroads which run along the western shore of the south branch were in its grasp. Now was the fire at its fiercest. Upward of 20 blocks were burning. Upward of 1,500 buildings, including outhouses, were on fire. Upward of 500 families were fleeing from the seeming wrath to come. The streets were almost impassable. Carriages, and wagons, and drays and carts, and all sorts of vehicles were brought into requisition, and were speedily loaded with household goods. Empty wagons were filled with freight, and where there were no beasts of burden to draw the load, human hands sprang to the rescue and dragged the property toward the north. Then the fire reached over the street, and while that terrible southwestern wind howled onward, it forced its way into the planing mills and the chair factories, and all the other shops which skirted the creek in that portion of west Chicago. Then it got into the lumber yards and into the railroad shops, and the round houses were soon wrapped in its dead embrace. The bricks themselves seemed only additional fuel. The rolling stock in the railroad yards seemed but a bit of kindling which helped along a fire already fiercely intense.

But worst of all the elevators were next in danger. For a few moments it seemed as though one or two of the largest would resist the flames and pass through the fire ordeal unscathed. But this thought was not of long duration, for an instant later and the immense piles were in flames from top to bottom.

Like the advance of a great army the fire moved forward in several columns, and like a powerless but unconquered foe the fire department slowly retreated. But they stubbornly contested every foot of ground and would not surrender, although often almost entirely surrounded by the dread enemy. Then they would cut their way out and retreat for a short distance, only to turn again and hurl their charges of thousands of gallons of water full into the face of the enemy. But no power on earth could stem the torrent. Never did firemen fight more fiercely to conquer, and never before did their heroic efforts seem so utterly in vain.

Suddenly away to the north and east, fully five blocks distant, a small flame broke forth and lighted up the already brilliant heavens. The sight sent an awful shudder to the soul of every man, woman and child who saw it. For a moment every one was spellbound and speechless.

Cash Assets,

Just where it was, the newly discovered fire, was as yet unknown, but it seemed to be in the neighborhood of the South Side gas works, and there was no one in all that vast concourse of people, but who knew the great danger which was already threatening the other side of the river. Every moment witnessed an increase in the blaze, and presently the outlines of the immense reservoir told the story of its immediate vicinity. The fire marshal at once sent every available engine to the south side, and prepared to follow with the remainder immediately. But the flames mounted higher and the fire grew fiercer, and spread itself out in all directions, until it was impossible to stay its further progress.

SOUTH DIVISION.

As early as twelve o'clock, the air of the extreme south division was hot with the fierce breath of the conflagration. The gale blew savagely, and upon its wings were borne pelting cinders, black driving smoke, blazing bits of timber, and glowing coals. These swept thickly over the river, drifting upon house-tops and drying the wooden buildings along the southern terminus of Market, Franklin, Adams, Monroe and Madison streets still closer to the combustion point for which they were already too well prepared.

The housetops were covered with anxious workers, and cistern streams, tubs and buckets were in constant use to subdue the flying bits of fire that were constantly clinging to shingles and cornices.

The First Foothold

obtained by the destroying angel in the south division was in the tar works adjacent to the gas works, just south of Adams street, and nearly opposite the armory. Almost instantaneously the structure was one livid sheet of flame, emitting a dense volume of thick black smoke that curtained this portion of the city as with the pall of doom. Faster than a man could walk, the flames leaped from house to house until fifth avenue (Wells street) was reached. A steamer or two were sent thither, but their previous experiences were only repeated, and no perceptible check was given to the onward progress of the flames. From the gas works to the point it had now reached, nearly the entire space was filled with small wooden structures, and their demolition was the work of but a few minutes.

The First Great Danger

apprehended from the ignition of the tar was of its communication to the gas works, and in less than ten minutes the entire establishment was on fire, the immense gasometer being completely surrounded by a wall of flame. The danger from its explosion drove the crowds away, and other scenes of equally absorbing interest occupying their attention, when the explosion came, it was witnessed by comparatively a few people, and was, it is believed, unaccompanied with any fatal results. The grand metre was apparently filled to about half its capacity. Its destruction did not occur until some three hours later.

Apparently but a few minutes subsequent to the ignition of the gas works, the wooden buildings south of the armory were found to be on fire, forming the apex of another widening track of desolation, and very soon joining with the other, the two uniting like twin demons of destruction, the armory helping to glut their fiendish cravings.

It may be of interest here to note the peculiarities of the wind currents and their strange effects. During all this time, as during the entire continuance of the fire, the wind was blowing a gale from a southwesterly direction, and above the tops of the buildings its course from midnight until 4 or 5 o'clock, varied but little, not veering more than one or two points of the compass. To the observer on the street, however, traversing the main thoroughfares and the alleys, the wind would seem to come from every direction. This is easily explained. New centres of intense heat were being continually formed, and the sudden rarification of the air in the different localities and its consequent displacement caused continually artificial currents, which swept around the corners and through the alleys in every direction, often with the fury of a tornado. This will account partly for the rapid widening of the tracks of devastation from their apex to the lake, as well as the phenomenon of the fire — to use a nautical phrase,—"eating into the wind."

THE GRAND PACIFIC HOTEL,

upon which the roof had but just been placed, and which, like the still-born child, was created only for the grave, was among the first of the better class of structures assaulted by the fire. Angered at its imposing front, and scorning the implied durability of its superb dimensions, the flames stormed relentlessly in, above, and around it, until, assured that it was at their absolute mercy, they left it tottering to the earth, and crawled luridly along the street in search of further prey. It was now that the waves of fire began to take upon themselves the mightiest of proportions.

How it was that, while even a hundred buildings might be blazing, others, far in advance of the track of the storm, could not be protected, has not been understood by those who were not despairingly following the course of destruction. It was partly on account of the artificial currents already mentioned, and because the huge tongues of flame actually stretched themselves out upon the pinions of the wind, for acres. Sheets of fire would reach over entire blocks, wrapping in every building inclosed by the four streets bounding them, and scarcely allowing the dwellers in the houses time to dash away unscorched. Hardly twenty minutes had elapsed from the burning of the Pacific hotel before the fire had cut its hot swath through every one of the magnificent buildings intervening, upon La Salle street, and had fallen mercilessly upon the Chamber of Commerce.

The few heroic workers of the police and fire departments who had not already dropped out of the ranks of fighters from sheer exhaustion, sought to once more check the progress of devastation by the aid of powder. A number of kegs were thrown into the basement of the grand business palace of the Merchants' Insurance company. A slow match was applied, and as the crowd drew back the explosion ensued. A broad, black chasm was opened in the face of the street, but with as little attention to the space intervening as though it had only been across an ordinary alley, the arms of flame swung over the gap, and tore lustily at the rows of banking houses and insurance structures beyond.

THE COURT HOUSE

was now faced with a swaying front of fire on the south and west sides. But as the building was in the centre of an open square, and solidly constructed, it was taken as a matter of course that it would be able to survive, if nothing else should be left standing around it.

"Talk about the Court House," said a leading banker, among the spectators, whose own establishment had already been melted to the very foundations, "it will show to be about the only sound building on the south side to-morrow."

And yet, in another five minutes, a great burning timber, wrenched from the tumbling ruins of a La Salle street edifice, had been hurled in wild fury at the wooden dome of the Court House. As if a thousand slaves of the fire-king had hidden within the fatal structure, awaiting this signal, the flames seemed to leap to simultaneous life in every part of the building, and soon the hot, scorched walls alone remained.

The course of the fire was now directed almost due east for a few minutes, and Hooley's opera house, *The Republican* office and the whole of Washington street to Dearborn was consumed.

CROSBY'S OPERA HOUSE

came next in order. Renovations to the extent of $80,000 had just been instituted in this edifice, and the place was to have been re-dedicated that same night by the Thomas orchestra. The combustible nature of the building caused it to burn with astonishing rapidity, and soon its walls surged in, carrying with them, among other treasures, the contents of three mammoth piano houses and a number of art treasures, including paintings by some of the leading masters of the old and new worlds.

The St. James hotel was next fired, and here, at the corner of State and Madison streets, the two savage currents of fire that had parted company near the Chamber of Commerce joined hideous issue once more. The course of one of these currents has been indicated. The other had swept down Franklin, Wells and La Salle streets to the main banks of the river, swallowing elevators, banks, trade palaces, the Briggs, Sherman, Tremont and other large hotels, Wood's museum, the beautiful structures of Lake and Randolph streets, and the entire surface comprised between Market, South Water, Washington and State streets.

Many lives were known to have been lost up to this time. But in the infernal furnace into which Chicago had been turned, it was impossible to conjecture or dare to imagine how many. The heat, more intense than anything that had ever been described in the annals of broadspread conflagrations of the past, had fairly crumbled to hot dust and ashes the heaviest of building stone. Of what chance was there then of ever finding the remains of lost humanity by those who were already inquiring, with mad anxiety, for the missing ones? But all thoughts of others soon began to vanish in fears for the safety of the living. The stoutest of masonry and thickest of iron had disappeared like wax before the blast.

Field & Leiter's magnificent store, second only in size and value of contents to one dry-goods house in the land, was already in flames. The streets were now crammed with vehicles conveying away valuables, and the sidewalks were running over with jostling men and women, all in a dazed, wild strife for the salvation of self, friends and property. The thieving horror had not yet broken out, and up to this time there had been a common, noble striving to aid the sufferers and stay the march of the furious flames.

Crackling and howling demoniacally at the ruin and misery left behind, eager for more valuable prey, the flames sped on, taking in their course—the track continually widening from the causes mentioned above—Farwell hall and the elegant stone structures surrounding it, and all the newspaper offices except that of *The Tribune*, leaving nothing behind but the grandest ruins the world ever saw.

The block bounded by Dearborn, Washington, State and Madison streets was some little time in burning. Indeed, after the corner occupied by the Union Trust and Savings institution had burned, it was believed that the large vacant lot created a short time before by the tearing down of the old Dearborn school, would save Mayo's corner and the St. Denis hotel. But the fire, in spite of the terrible strength of the wind in the other direction, eventually contrived to beat up against the gale, and, by devouring the stores of Gossage and others, on the west side of State, and the book houses of Griggs, Keen & Cooke, and the Western News company, on the east side, to blister the St. Denis to the igniting point, and then McVicker's theatre and *The Tribune* building formed the northern boundary of the south division.

It was here that the few workers now left with courage enough to contest with miserable fortune made their final stand. *The Tribune* building was believed to be fire-proof if any structure devised by man could be proof against such a combination of the elements as was now raging.

THE POSTOFFICE

had yielded to the assault and was only a smouldering ruin, and from away down to the devastated depot of the Illinois Central the flames had pushed back until they interlocked once more at the custom-house with the fire that had torn its way from the Michigan Central depot. Surrounded by

THE ENEMY ON EVERY QUARTER,

and having held proudly up against the attack till long after daybreak, there was the same sad capitulations enacted here that had been the story of the entire night. McVicker's yielded first and was instantly a heap of brick and ashes, and *The Tribune* structure was not long in following, the walls of this latter structure, with those of the Custom House, First National bank, and Court House proving the most stubborn evidences of the worth of the architect's skill remaining in Chicago. Up to this time, the elegant and costly row of buildings on Dearborn street north of the Postoffice had escaped. They included the two Honore structures, the Bigelow house, which was soon to have been opened, and the DeHaven block, the latter extending from Quincy to Jackson street. The two blocks bounded by Monroe, State, Jackson and Dearborn streets, that resting on Jackson street, including the Palmer house and the Academy of Design, were also intact. A new line of flame, however, had been formed some distance to the southward of the armory and west of the Michigan Southern depot, and was sweeping on in its mad, resistless career, and it was felt that the above mentioned property was in the greatest peril.

THE DEPOT,

a noble stone structure, upon which great reliance was placed for the safety of the adjacent property to the eastward, made but a feeble resistance, and soon, with a large number of passenger cars inside, was in ruins. The large row of wooden tenements on Griswold street, fronting the depot on the east, succumbed at once, presenting a wall of fire of the length of the depot. It burned rapidly through to Third avenue, but at that point the wind, which had begun to show a changeableness it had not previously exhibited, veered to a point considerably east of south, in which quarter it remained for some time. Encouraged by this,

A DESPERATE FIGHT

was made on Third avenue, and for some minutes, minutes that seemed hours in the torturing alternations of hope and fear, the fiery monster was held at bay. The stone yards on La Salle street also temporarily checked the progress of the fire south. Thousands of people occupying the large tract from Third avenue and Dearborn street to the lake watched, with anxious countenances and bated breath, the result of the battle that was to decide the fate of their homes. The wind benignly continued to blow from the same quarter, and the hopes that had been raised, slight at first, grew stronger. It was

An Awful Crisis.

At no period in the history of that terrible day were more momentous interests trembling in the balance. The occupants of the Michgan avenue palaces and the humble cottagers were there side by side, breathing supplications and agonizing prayers that their hearthstones might be spared.

The Christian Brothers' school, at the corner of Van Buren street and Third avenue, a massive brick structure, was soon ignited, but its walls proved sound and strong, and the interior was almost entirely burned before they fell. New hopes were born of this, but only to be succeeded by the blankest despair.

And the suspense was not for long. Making a clean skip over the DeHaven block, a shower of fire-brands, hurled thither by a treacherous gust of wind, alighted on the roof of the Bigelow house, and that magnificent building was soon a seething furnace of flame, quickly followed by the two Honore buildings.

The one nearest the Bigelow hotel was unfinished, but was rapidly approaching completion, and as a model of architectural beauty was hardly rivaled in the city.

From these buildings, as if maddened at their slight detention, the flames spread to the standing buildings west and southwest with redoubled fury, enwrapping the block containing the Palmer house and Academy of Design, and that directly north, in an inconceivably short time.

The Palmer house was the tallest building in the city, eight stories high, three of which were in its mansard roof, and the scene of its demolition, which was more rapid than the account can be transmitted to paper, was inexpressibly grand. The march of the devouring element from this point to the lake was uninterrupted, the intervening buildings, including many of the finest private residences in the city, melting away like the dry stubble of the prairie.

For some time after the ignition of the Bigelow house, the DeHaven block stood unscathed, but at last, it, too, was forced to yield to the inevitable. It was a long three-story building, the opposite side of Dearborn street being occupied by a row of small wooden tenements. A stream was brought to bear upon these, and in the blistering heat three firemen, heroes every one, fully conscious of the tremendous interests committed to them, stood manfully at their posts. They did their work nobly and successfully. The DeHaven block was levelled to the ground and the whole row of wooden buildings had been perfectly protected. From a thousand parched throats the thankful ejaculation went up; "We are saved!" Delusive hope! One danger was averted only to be succeeded by others beyond the power of man to avert. The wind again suddenly turned to the southwest carrying with it a baptism of fire which made it apparent that the whole remaining portion of the city north of Harrison street was doomed. Churches, palatial residences,

everything was swept by the besom of destruction, an irresistible avalanche of flame.

In concert with the work of devastation just described, from the track of flame several blocks below, which had long before cut its way to the lake, as if executing a well-devised military manœuvre, the fire had been steadily eating its way against the wind, the point of junction being at, or near Adams street. From this it was evident that, even with the wind blowing a gale from the south, the entire south division was in danger. The supply of water had long before failed, except from the basin.

A More Heroic Treatment

alone could save what remained of the city. It was at once and unhesitatingly determined upon, and then commenced the first systematic and thorough use of gunpowder as the only means of preventing the continuance of the work of ruin. It was conducted under the personal supervision of Gen. Sheridan. Building after building was demolished, the reports of the successive explosions coming at intervals of a very few moments, and being plainly audible above the continuous din, each discharge announcing that at last the battle was being fought and won. The great fire which was to render Chicago forever memorable in the annals of history was ended in the south division.

The Last Building to Burn

was "Terrace row," a palatial block of private residences on Michigan avenue, extending northward from Harrison street. Its destruction required two or three hours, as nothing remained in its rear to accelerate the work. About eighteen hours from the first discovery of the fire on De Koven street, the last wall of "Terrace row" fell. In the south division, north of a diagonal line, reaching from the east end of Harrison street to Polk street bridge, there remained two buildings unharmed, one the large business block immediately north of Randolph street bridge, and the other an unfinished stone structure at the corner of Monroe and La Salle streets. The entire business portion of the city was obliterated. Two-thirds of the territorial area of the city was unscathed, but Chicago, as a great business mart, the proud commercial centre of the growing west, was no more. Was ever devastation more complete!

Immense as is the burnt area in the south division, for a single fortunate circumstance it might, and probably would, have been doubled. Immediately south of the Michigan Southern passenger depot was a long, fire-proof warehouse; on the side fronting the fire, there were but two windows, which afforded the only possible opportunity for the fire fiend to effect a lodgment. These were successfully guarded by a small corps of men with pails. The building was saved, and with it, undoubtedly, the entire tract north of Twelfth street.

NORTH DIVISION.

The north side, in proportion to its size, perhaps suffered more than both of the other divisions united. Practically, with the exception of a few streets, which were occupied by retail stores to a certain extent, as Clark and Wells streets, and also North Water and Kinzie streets, which were occupied by wholesale stores, commission merchants, wholesale butchers, manufactories, etc., and a narrow strip along the north branch occupied by lumber and coal yards, the north side was almost exclusively a residence portion of the city. In the extent of territory burned, north Chicago was also the most unfortunate. Doubly unfortunate, also, was it in the fact that when the fire once started north of the river its progress was entirely unchecked, all the fire engines being at work on the south side, from whence they could not reach the north side, even if they would, except by a long detour around by Twelfth street and the west division,— a raging barrier of flame making it impossible for the engines to pass over either the Lake street, Randolph street, Madison street, or Adams street bridges to the west side, and so from that side over the Kinzie street bridge and other bridges north of that bridge. In addition to this, the north side was unfortunate in that its population, moving almost block by block as the flames progressed north, were at last compelled, with the exception of a comparatively few families, to sleep out all night on the open prairie, which environs the north division on the west and north; the fire not ceasing its march of desolation until it had devoured all but a narrow strip of houses on the west side of that portion of the north division which lies north of Division street.

The Commencement

of the fire on the north side seems to have been at the Galena elevator, which is located on the north side of the main branch between State street and Rush street, the time when it first crossed over being about 20 minutes to 6 o'clock in the morning. Having once got a start to the north of the river, the fire rapidly progressed north, east, and west, the back-fire west being unusually rapid. The corner of Rush aud Illinois streets, three blocks beyond the elevator, where Judge Grant Goodrich resided, was soon reached.

Business Portion Burned.

The fire then, as above intimated, progressed rapidly west, as well as north and east, first burning down the old Lake house, one of the oldest, if not the oldest, brick hotel in Chicago. In its course west, it also burned down, in addition to the other buildings, old St. James' church, the oldest brick church in Chicago, which was occupied as a storehouse. About this time, other portions of the north side adjoining the river caught fire, and soon all North Water street, which was occupied by wholesale stores and large wholesale markets, was in flames, the

Galena depot, the Hough house, on Wells street, and the Wheeler elevator, west of Wells street, being also burned down.

THE NORTH SIDE BRIDGES

also were rapidly burned up, the flames from them helping to communicate the fire rapidly all along the north shore of the main branch. Not a bridge connecting the north side with the south side was left; Wells street bridge, Clark street bridge, State street bridge, Rush street bridge, all were burned.

Between Kinzie street and the river all was laid low and buried in a mass of undistinguishable ruins. Uhlich's hall, the Ewing block, the Galena depot, the offices of the Northwestern company, at the corner of Wells and Kinzie streets, the Galena elevator, all were burned down in a miraculously short space of time.

Between Kinzie street and Illinois street, from the north branch to the lake, nearly all was burned; among the prominent buildings consumed being the Revere house, on the northeast corner of Kinzie and Clark, the North Market hall, one of the oldest buildings in Chicago, the Lake house, one of the oldest brick structures in the city, the mammoth reaper factory of McCormick & Co., a large sugar refinery, and an extensive coal yard; the last three establishments being located east of Rush street.

A FEW FORTUNATE BUILDINGS

were left standing, but they only seemed to emphasize the ruins around them. These exceptions were about a block of buildings extending west from Market street to the north branch, on the north side of Kinzie street, and a large brick building, occupied as a stove warehouse by Rathbone & Co., located to the south of Ogden slip on the land which has been made between it and the slip, and which extends out into the lake several hundred feet.

Between Illinois street and Chicago avenue the fire progressed with irrepressible fury and rapidity, soon enveloping the whole section, including in it both the most beautiful and the most forbidding portions of the north division. On the west of Clark street and south of Chicago avenue was a section of the city densely populated; filled with buildings occupied, many of them, by two and three families; a region which in years gone by was noted for the disorderly character of its elections. Its only prominent features were a few churches, including the German Lutheran church, on the corner of La Salle and Ohio streets, and a Norwegian Lutheran church, built in 1855, on the corner of Superior and Franklin streets; the Kinzie school, a four story brick building, on Ohio street, between La Salle and Wells; the fine large structure known as the German house, dedicated last year, and containing one of the finest and best proportioned halls in the city. This portion of the city had, in fact, just begun to renovate itself; its streets were being raised and graded, and new buildings erected.

East of Clark street to the lake, between Illinois street and Chicago avenue, was the pride of the north division. Its streets were bordered with rows of magnificent trees, beautiful gardens, elegant mansions, noble churches, all of which fell before the destroyer. Among the churches were the North Presbyterian church, an immense brick structure, on the corner of Indiana and Cass streets; a couple of frame churches on Dearborn street; the new St. James church, a beautiful gothic stone structure, on the corner of Huron and Cass streets, and the vast structure of the cathedral of the Holy Name, on the corner of State and Superior streets. Among the other prominent public buildings were the Catholic college of St. Mary of the Lake, occupying the whole block north of the cathedral of the Holy Name; the Orphans home, conducted by Sisters of Mercy; the Historical society's building on Ontario street, east of Clark, in which were kept among many other valuable historical records, the original proclamation of emancipation by President L ncoln, and the north-side police station on Huron street, between Clark and Dearborn streets, a substantial and well-arranged building. Among the prominent residnces were those of Mrs. Walter L. Newberry, whose grounds occupied the whole block bounded by Ontario, Rush, Pine and Erie streets; that of Isaac N. Arnold, occupying the block north; that of McGee, occupying the block southwest of the Ogden block, etc. In short, this section of the north division was full of beautiful residences and gardens.

In the northeast corner of this section was the vast building of Lill's ale and lager beer brewery, occupying the two blocks bounded on the south by Superior street, on the north by Chicago avenue, on the west by Pine street, and on the east by the lake,—the whole of the two blocks being occupied by the brewery, except a small slip on the southwest corner of Pine and Superior streets, and a small portion occupied by the residence of Mr. Lill. In the western of the two blocks were the ice house, the malt house, the brewing house, etc., all substantial and elegant brick buildings; the eastern block or rather block and a half were occupied by stables, carpenter shop, cooper shop, blacksmith shop, etc., several of which were built out over the lake on piles.

The Chicago Water Works.

Before tracing the progress of the fire further northward must be mentioned the burning of the water works, and the curious or rather incomprehensible manner in which it caught fire almost two hours before the time that the fire first reached the north division across the main branch. As stated above, the Galena elevator at the edge of the main branch caught fire from the south side at about 20 minutes to 6 o'clock. At about 20 minutes before 4 o'clock, fire was discovered in the carpenter shop of Mr. Lill, built on piles above the shallow water of the lake. The employes at the brewery immediately endeavored to extinguish the flames, but it was found impossible, and all the efforts of the men were confined to prevent their extension. Standing between the burning carpenter shop and the water works, extending northwest of the shop, stood one of Mr. Lill's bookkeepers. Turning round toward the water works, he exclaimed, "My God, the water works are in flames." This gentleman states positively that the flames from the water works, when he first saw them, were issuing from the western portion of the pumping works, no flames being seen from the eastern portion of the grounds, which were occupied with coal sheds, etc. On the other hand, the employes at the water works say that the fire commenced about half-past 3 o'clock in the morning; that it commenced in the eastern part of the water works, and that it took fire from the shed. Another gentleman testifies that the carpenter shop or the cooper shop, as he called it, was burned down before the fire commenced in the water works, and that when the water works were in full flame the main body of Lill's brewery, with the exception of the carpenter shop, was intact. The time of the commencement of the fire in Lill's carpenter shop and the water works, however, differs one hour; the last named witness asserting that the water works commenced burning at about half-past 2 or 3 o'clock, The whole building was soon in flames, and in a few minutes the engineers had to rush out of the building to save their lives. The machinery was very considerably injured. The water tower, however, to the west of the pumping works, was almost entirely uninjured.

On the Sands.

Before relating the further progress of the flames northward, must also be noticed the mingled scenes of sorrow and laughter, or tragedy and comedy, which were presented on what were once known as the sands—that part of the lake shore which lies east of that portion of the north side which has been described above. This sandy waste varies in width between one and two blocks, being the widest at the southern end, near the river, where a frame building stood here and there before the fire. As soon as the fire broke out along the north side of the main river, and the rapidity of its progress showed that it would sweep the north side, or a considerable portion of it, all the inhabitants of the district described, lying east of State street, — both rich and poor, both the tenants of the shanties and cottages which occupied North Water street, Michigan street, Illinois street, and the south end of St. Clair street, and the tenants of the aristocratic mansions north of this locality,—fled to the lake shore, carrying with them whatever they were able to carry in their hands, but little and but short opportunity being offered to do more. The scene was one of indescribable confusion, of horror and dismay, intermingled to the mere spectator with laughable incidents, which were, however, quickly drowned in the overwhelming horror which surrounded them all. Where the lake shore, or sands, were narrow, and the burning buildings approached close to the lake shore, despair reigned. The water was the apparent boundary of the place of refuge. The intense heat from the burning buildings, even the flames from them, reached the water, and even stretched out over it, and the flying men, women, and children, rushed into the lake till nothing but their heads appeared above the surface of the waters; but the fiery fiend was not satisfied. The hair was burned off the heads of many, while some never came out of the water alive. Many who stayed on the shore, where the space between the fire and water was a little wider, had the clothes burned from off their backs.

Those again who lived west of Clark street in the district named, as soon as they saw that they must succumb to the advancing flames, after flying, and moving north their goods from block to block, rushed across the bridges which, with one exception, that of the Chicago avenue bridge,—remained standing. There was a grand emigration, to the west side, of people and goods; of little children and big; of crying women and excited men; of broken furniture and cracked crockery; of wheelbarrows, buggies, one-horse teams, two-horse teams, heavy wagons, and light wagons,—everything that could be saved.

What was saved in the district south of Chicago avenue, except what has already been mentioned, was located on the banks of the river. The property saved from the flames was as follows: The new north-side gas works just south of the Chicago avenue bridge, the old works south of that being burned; a litle lumber yard just south of Erie street, which was partially built on piles into the river; several coal yards along Kingsbury street, which runs along the river side at a distance of about half a block. The coal yard of Blake, Whitehouse & Co., was saved almost entire, a large, cheap frame building in which coal was piled up being alone destroyed. Next north of this was Reno & Little's coal yard. Here most of the coal was saved, though nothing was left of several large piles but the cinders. Several small frame buildings on Kingsbury street, between Indiana and Kinzie streets, are only partially burned and can be repaired. Holbrook's and Dewey & Co.'s coal yards to the east of Kingsbury street, and Brown & Van Arsdale's Manufacturing company's building were also left uninjured to any serious extent.

North of Chicago Avenue.

At this time, between five and half-past five, the line of the fire as it progressed north, was about a mile in width. Along the entire line the fire appeared as if attempting to see which portion could surpass the other in its march of destruction. To the east, near the lake shore, were the large ale and lager beer breweries of Sands, Huck, Brandt, Bowman, Schmidt, Busch, Doyle, etc.; to the west, near the north branch, was a densely-inhabited district filled with wooden houses as dry as tinder. From the three, four and five stories' height of the one, the sparks and burning charcoal from the wooded cupolas of the breweries were blown blocks northward, setting fire to the buildings on which they fell. On the west, the closely-built wooden frame buildings, having no brick walls to temporarily stay their progress, seemed to surrender instantaneously to the raging fire fiend that did not crawl but seemed to rush upon them with unrestrainable fury.

All seemed to be immersed in a hell of flame. No attempts were made to stem the progress of the fire. All that the tenants of the houses could do was to save a few of their household goods, and this, too, at the risk of their lives. The scene was rendered still more appalling by the fact that during the earlier stages of the fire, thousands of the able-bodied men had rushed to the south side to witness the fire there, not then dreaming that it would reach their own homes. Before the fire on the south side, these fathers, brothers and sons, were gradually driven across the river, until the rapidity of the progress of the flames convinced them that their own families were in danger. Being at last convinced, they rushed in frantic haste to save what little they could. But they arrived at their homes, most of them, in an exhausted condition. They did their best, but the best was but little. All that many could do was to aid in saving the lives of the'r wiv.s and children. With their all, standing in their houses, many attempted impossible things, and rushed into burning buildings never to come out alive; for the wind rushed on in horrible fury, and seemed to envelop three or four houses at once in one fell swoop.

Until the densely-populated district to the west of La Salle street and between Chicago avenue and North avenue had been wasted, there was no stay to the rapid progress of the fire. All that many people could do was to save themselves, and perhaps a few valuables that they could carry in their hands. A few indeed, ot those who saw beforehand that their homes would be burned down, even when the flames were half a mile off, saved, perhaps, half of their furniture; but many of these even were able to save but little. No conveyance could be found in many cases, and piles of furniture were only saved from the house to be burned in the street. East of Dearborn street the scene was a parallel one; the homeless occupants of the houses in many cases rushing to the narrow beach which bounds this portion of the north division on the east, and the same sufferings that occurred on the portion of the beach referred to south of this, were repeated and aggravated by the narrowness of the beach. How many were killed, how many dangerously burned, it will be impossible to find out. Relatives and friends have not waited for the coroner, but have buried their own dead on their own responsibility, and no one person will ever know the names, or even the number, of the victims of the fire in the north division. In the district mentioned, with the exception of La Salle street, Clark street, and Dearborn street, the population was densely packed. In many of the houses lived two or three families. To the east of it were large breweries, where, till the last moment, the employes worked to save the buildings, at last rushing to their own already burning buildings to save their families. Children, as is usual in poor districts, seemed to swarm around every building,

and how many of these, left to their own care, infants, toddling children, little boys and girls, sank before the fire it is impossible to estimate. Suffice it to say that hundreds have been missed who were seen at the fire but never since.

A Fortunate District.

That portion of the north division which lies between Chestnut street and Oak street, and between La Salle street and Dearborn street, was remarkably fortunate. The only house in the north division inside the limits of the fire that has escaped not only destruction but even injury, is located in this district. This house is that of Mahlon D. Ogden, Esq., on the north side of the street variously known as Whiting and Whitney streets and Lafayette place. Undoubtedly the saving of this house from the flames was due to the fact that south of it was the Washington park, or square, and on the south-west and west the two blocks, occupied, the southern by Mr. McCagg, and the northern by the widow of a rich citizen. On each of the last two named blocks only one house stood. The house on the latter block was almost entirely destroyed. The house on the block to the south was but partially destroyed, and the large hot-house to the south of it, and one of the finest in the city, was hardly injured at all, but a few panes of glass on the north side of it being broken by the heat. Among other buildings burned was the Ogden school, near State street.

Lincoln Park and Old City Cemetery.

These deserve special mention. Lincoln park—the glory of the north division—has been almost entirely preserved. But few trees have been injured, except in the southeastern portion of the park where the dead house stood and where a few trees are burned; the small-pox hospital to the east on the lake shore being also destroyed. The gravestones or rather board memorials of the dead poor are many of them destroyed, and their relatives will know no more the place of rest of their kindred. The fences around the graves, the boards which have told to the wanderer their names, are all destroyed in the southern portion of the old cemetery. In the park itself many took refuge, though the great majority, as hereafter stated, fled to the prairies on the northwest.

North of North avenue no efforts whatever were made to stop the progress of the flames, with one exception, which will be hereafter mentioned. They followed out their course, the only means that prevented their progress both north and west being stretches of bare prairie on which there was nothing to burn. Excepting on Clark and Wells streets, the houses were more or less separated from each other, occupying or being separated from each other by two or three lots and often more. A small portion of the district north of North avenue and west of Wells street was thickly settled.

The Northern Limit of the Fire.

At Fullerton avenue, a little over two-and-a-half miles north of the

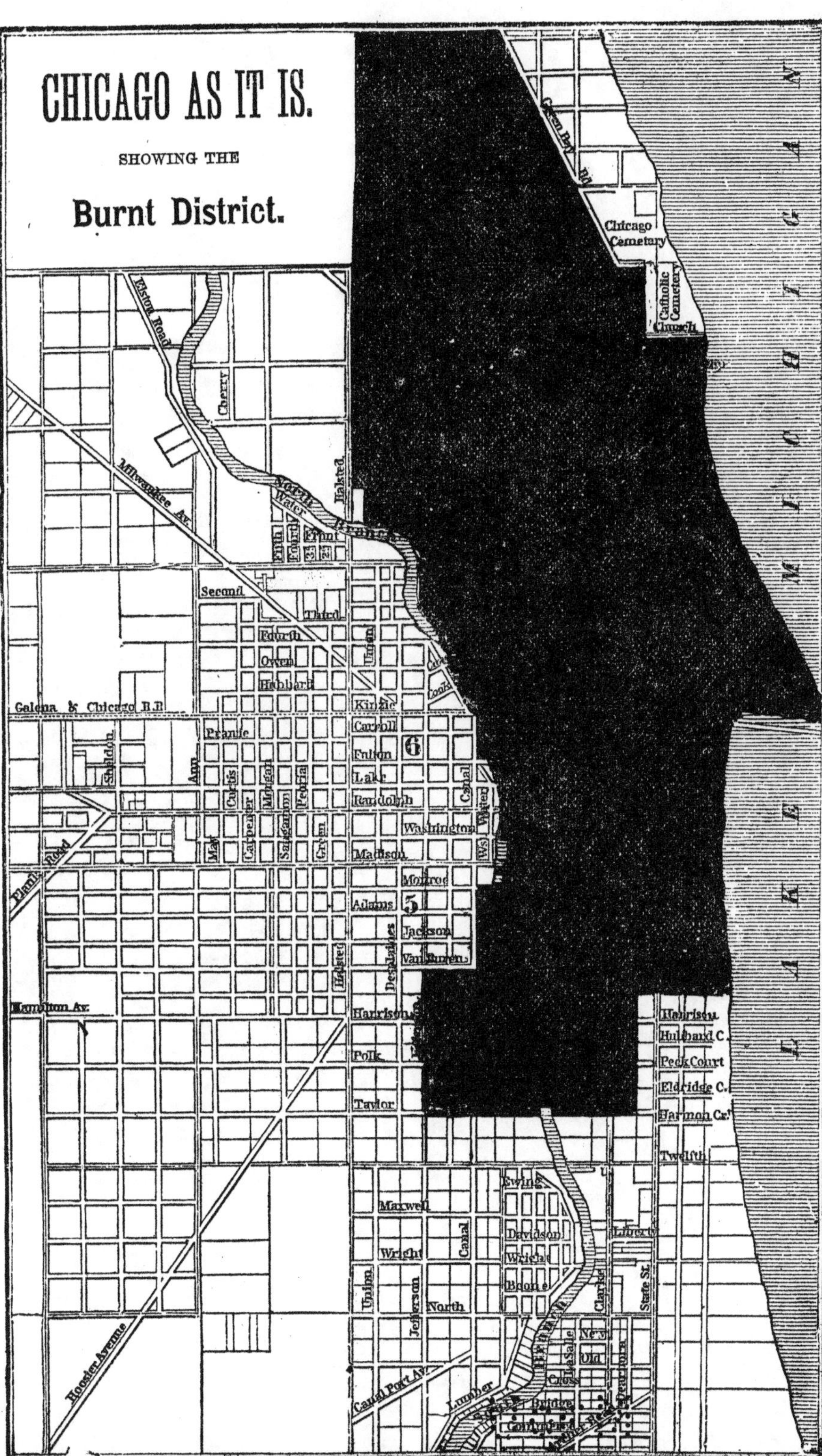
CHICAGO AS IT IS.
SHOWING THE
Burnt District.
LAKE MICHIGAN
Chicago Cemetary
Catholic Cemetery
Milwaukee Av.
Cherry
Halsted
Second
Third
Fourth
Owen
Hubbard
Galena & Chicago R.R.
Kinzie
Carroll
Fulton
Lake
Randolph
Washington
Madison
Monroe
Adams
Jackson
Van Buren
Harrison
Polk
Taylor
Twelfth
Maxwell
Wright
North
Canal
Union
Jefferson
Sheldon
Ann
May
Curtis
Carpenter
Morgan
Sangamon
Peoria
Green
Desplaines
Plank Road
Hamilton Av.
Hoosier Avenue
Canal Port Av.
Lumber
Harrison
Hubbard C.
Peck Court
Eldridge C.
Harmon Ct.
Ewing
Davidson
Liberty
Clarke
State St.
Cross
Old
New
Dearborn
6
5

river, the progress of the fire was finally stopped. A lull of the wind, between two and four o'clock on Tuesday morning, aided in the work of preventing the further progress of the flames northward; the only houses burned north of Fullerton avenue being Mr. John Huck's residence, and a building occupied by a Mr. Felk. Between the hours named Mr. Huck's men turned out and beat out the sparks that came from the south as they fell on the ground. A slight rain falling at the same time aided in the work.

A Night on the Prairie.

During all this time, however, that the fire had been raging in the north division, sometimes advancing directly northeast, sometimes progressing westward with a terrible back-fire, people had been flying north and northwest, until the few houses within reach in Lake View and beyond the limits were crowded full of refugees, and the flying population were compelled to take refuge on the open prairie. Here were gathered thousands of people, tired men, delicate women, children in arms without cover, without shelter of any kind; many, indeed, without clothes on their backs. Worse than all, here, too, were compelled to rest from their long-continued flight, the sick and the wounded.

And as if these experiences were not enough to satisfy the demon of destruction that had driven them hither, women were seized with the pains of childbirth, and children were born on the open prairie. The scene was a sorrowful one. Even water was denied to the parched lips of the unexpected wanderers upon the prairies.

Boundaries of the Fire on the North Side.

The boundaries of the fire in the north division were as follows: With the exception of the few buildings mentioned above, the fire extended over all the north division from the main branch to Division street, and from the north branch to the lake; very nearly 700 acres of territory. The fire left the north branch at Division street, where it left a few houses standing along the side of the river. The back-fire then extended to the river again, or to what is known as the north-branch canal, which connects the ends of a semi-circle in the river, which bends over to the west. Following the canal, or new channel of the river, for a short distance, the fire then tended a little to the east, as far as Halsted street, up which it extended to Clybourne avenue, the back-fire extending along the avenue northwest to Blackhawk street, and a little west until it reached Orchard street—a north and south street, excepting at its junction with the avenue, where it runs for about a block in a northeast direction. After reaching Orchard street, the fire proceeded north to Willard street, where it proceeded east along Howe street to Hurlbut street, across a couple of undivided blocks. Along Hurlbut street the fire proceeded north to Centre avenue, on which only three houses were burned down; the blocks around being nearly vacant. It then advanced up Hurlbut street to within about 100 feet of Fullerton avenue. In the meanwhile the fire had taken all east of this with the exception of Lincoln park. North of Fullerton avenue, the fire burned up only two houses; those being located east of Clark street. Here the progress of the fire was stayed in the manner stated above.

BETWEEN FIRE AND WATER.

No narrative could possess more terrible interest than that which should tell, in the simplest words, the story of the many wonderful escapes from death in the awful conflagration of Chicago. That many persons perished in the burning is already known. That the number may have been hundreds is possible. God alone can ever knew the manner or the agonies of their death. But of thousands of those who escaped from the awful cyclone of fire, the story is one that finds hardly a parallel in all human experience since the world begun.

The greater number of these

Terrible Experiences

occurred in the north division. The more combustible nature of the buildings in that part of the city gave to the conflagration a wider sweep and a more rapid movement than in the south division. Like a mighty line of battle, the conflagration extended its terrible banners of flame until the right rested on the lake; the left on the river; then advancing in one awful charge, it literally swept that portion of the city from the face of the earth. Nothing could penetrate that vast line of flame and live. Before it 60,000 men, women and children fled for their lives.

On the eastern side of the district, many persons fled to the lake shore, supposing that to be a place of entire safety. Many, indeed, were cut off by the rapidly advancing flames from the possibility of escape in any other direction. For nearly all who sought escape in that direction the sequel proved that they had taken a fearful chance.

The experience of Mr. Lambert Tree and family was in part that of many. Perceiving that his own house could not escape, Mr. Tree, with his wife and child and aged father, went to the residence of his father-in-law, Mr. Magee. The Magee residence occupied the centre of a large enclosure, and was therefore regarded as a place of probable safety. But the very fact that of its isolation from surrounding buildings soon revealed that it was the most dangerous retreat that could have been chosen. The conflagration enveloped it completely on all sides before the house took fire. On the side opposite to the approaching flames, the square was enclosed by a high board fence, without openings. On the front, the flames had already cut off all possibility of retreat. The only way of escape was toward the northeast, over the fence already mentioned; a barrier which three aged persons, a woman already fainting in the dense smoke, and a little child half suffocated, could not possibly scale. The fence, too, was on fire.

The house was already enveloped in a shower of burning fire-brands. A horrible death seemed to be the inevitable doom of the entire party.

At this terrible juncture, a portion of the burning fence fell to the ground, opening a gateway from the fiery *cul de sac.* Through this opening, Mr. Tree, dragging his fainting wife and child, fled toward the lake. In the flight from the premises the party became separated. Nothing more was seen of Mr. and Mrs. Magee until, on the following day, they were found on the prairie northwest of the city. In their flight, they had taken a different direction from the others, and had no choice but to hasten on before the advancing fire until beyond the line of its horrible path. The aged couple passed the night of Monday on the open prairie.

In an open space, sheltered by the walls of Lill's brewery, Mr. Tree and his family, with some of their neighbors, again supposed themselves to be in a place of safety. But from this refuge they were also driven by the advancing flames. The intense heat drove them to the beach, and even into the water, in which many men, women and children stood for an hour, throwing water over their clothing to prevent it taking fire from the flame and sparks which a fierce wind drove toward them. In one instance the dress of a lady actually took fire; the wearer, with great presence of mind, removed it from her person to the lake. The heat, ever and anon, enveloped the fugitives like hot blasts from the mouth of a furnace. Dense clouds of stifling smoke swept over them, threatening instant suffocation. Children fainted, and strong men could only breathe by keeping their faces to the ground until some new air current, lifting the smoke or turning aside the fiery blast, gave temporary relief. The situation is described by those who experienced its horrors, as one surpassing all possibilities of conception or belief. But the flames, finding at length no more to consume, swept on and the fugitives were saved.

LOSS AND INSURANCE.

It is impossible to ascertain in dollars and cents the precise amount of the loss; it is not, however, impossible to make a trustworthy approximation, from actual and unimpeachable data.

And, preliminary thereto, it may be well to say that the ten thousand guesses at the aggregate loss which one hears in every place are mostly of the wildest and absurd character. The aggregate loss has been variously guessed to be two, three, four, five, and so on to eight or nine hundred millions of dollars. One will meet in an hour's walk among the ruins twenty intelligent men who will avow that not a dollar less than $500,000,000 of property has been destroyed. This is nonsense. At the most liberal estimate $500,000,000 would cover the value of every particle of property of every kind that ever existed within the corporate limits of Chicago. It is certainly not all destroyed; nor a half, nor a third of it.

A CAREFUL CALCULATION

will show that $150,000,000 is a liberal estimate for the value that has been destroyed by the conflagration. The valuation of property for city taxation for the present year was in round numbers as follows:

REAL ESTATE (INCLUDING BUILDINGS.)

South Division	$110,000,000
West Division	87,000,000
North Division	38,000,000
Total	$235,000,000

PERSONAL PROPERTY.

South Division	$40,000,000
West Division	8,000,000
North Division	5,000,000
Total	$53,000,000

The judgment of the most trustworthy experts is that the assessed valuation of real property is rather over than under two-thirds of the actual cash value, upon an average of the whole city, while that of personal property is probably rather under than over one-third of the actual cash value. Adding one-third to the real property and two-thirds to the personal, and the total value of all property in the city of Chicago before the fire was $469,000,000. How much of this value still remains? How much of it has the fire destroyed?

Assessment District No. 1 included all the south division north of Twelfth street. The total valuation of land and buildings in that district was $64,000,000; about $40,000,000 for the former, and $24,000,000 for the latter. Much the greater part of the personal property of the south division was in that district; probably $35,000,000; total $99,000,000. Deducting $40,000,000 for the land, and the loss, if everything else were destroyed, would be $60,000,000, according to the assessor's valuation; or if this be equal upon an average of real and personal estate to one-half the actual cash value (which is believed to be quite within the fact), an actual loss of $120,000,000. Similarly, the actual loss in the north division is found to be in the vicinity of $30,000,000. But from this calculation must be deducted all that unburnt portion of assessment district No. 1, between Twelfth and Harrison streets, and a small unburnt district in the northwest corner of the north division. From it must also be deducted the value of all personal property saved from the fire. To it must be added the loss in the burnt district of the west division. Thus, while the calculation does not assume the character of precision, it furnishes a trustworthy approximation, showing that $150,000,000 will cover the entire destruction of property by the conflagration.

A SURVEY BY STREETS.

No better idea of the losses can be obtained than can be got by going over a little in detail the area swept by the fire in the south division. As yet, and for weeks and months to come, no one will be able to enumerate these losses accurately and elaborately.

Beginning not with the point where the fire commenced, but at the main branch of the river for convenience, let us enumerate the streets and, as far as possible, recall what was on them, what was bought and sold and stored there, and by whom they were occupied.

And first, South Water street was swept with destruction's besom, from the south branch to the lake. Here went down the lumber exchange, several elevators with their contents, almost innumerable houses stored with flour, with apples and butter, with lard and pork, poultry, farm products, garden vegetables, and on the east half of the street on both sides were wholesale houses stored from cellar to attic with groceries, coarse and fine, with the products of Europe, the wines of Burgundy and the Rhine; coffees from South America, the West Indies, and the Orient; teas piled high like a Canton storehouse; whiskies, the distilled essence of thousands of acres of Illinois corn,—these, with all that was left of the Fort Dearborn buildings, were wiped out, for the entire length of the street, with the peculiar paraphernalia of the street, the skids, the clogged and choked sidewalks, through which buyers wended sinuous. Where, now, oh consignees from the northwest, are the products of your labor! You may come in thousands, as you already have, to look after them; but they are consigned where no consignee or purchaser will ever see them,—into oxygen and hydrogen, thin air.

While pursuing its resistless way a.ong this street, eating through the vegetables, and poultry, and fruits, and provisions of the northwest more rapidly than the carnivorous tooth of time aided by the forces of decay, the fires were also sweeping across the river.

Next take Lake street. This street, which for twenty years has stood as the great business street of Chicago, was totally destroyed from end to end, from the lake to the river, with the contents of the houses. The principal hide and leather houses occupied the west end; next came several heavy hardware and cutlery establishments, farm implement establishments and toy shops, some of the largest silver and plated ware establishments, clothing houses, large retail dry goods houses, and below Dearborn street both sides of the street were occupied for about a quarter of a mile with palatial marble-fronted rows where goods where only sold at wholesale; tall buildings whose shadows fell entirely across the street and terminated somewhat up the fronts of the opposite side. These, containing millions of dollars' worth of goods of all kinds, the labor of the loom, from sunny France, from Italy, from India and China, and the shops of old and of new England, were all consigned at last to the general limbo of total destruction. At the foot of this street stood several fine hotels, the Adams, the Richmond and Massasoit houses and the great railroad union depot, a marvel of magnitude and art, whose picture graces some of the school geographies. These, with the freight buildings and the warehouses beyond almost to the mouth of the harbor, containing freight and stores, and grain in quantities that nobody knows, and probably never will, in the aggregate, were all consumed.

Then Randolph street followed. The Lind block stands, at the bridge, the solitary structure left out of all that was valuable, beautiful, or grand on this street. This was the street where the large hotels stood, the Sherman house, the Briggs house, the Metropolitan, the Matteson, and several others. A large number of furniture establishments and toy establishments occupied the west end of the street, while the east end was devoted, like Lake street, to wholesale houses, including the great auction houses, the Museum, the Northwestern Engraving company's building, and several wholesale grocery establishments, together with a miscellaneous business, comprising retail establishments, banks, etc., which were all consigned to ruin with the rest.

Washington street, from the tunnel to the lake, comprised many of the best buildings in the city. It was largely devoted to banks, offices, insurance, and real estate dealers. On this street was the Second Presbyterian church, the Union bank building, the Merchants' insurance building, the Nevada house, the Opera house, St. James' hotel, the First National bank, the Board of Trade, and a large number of other equally fine blocks, almost all of which were marble fronts.

Then all of Madison street, from the lake to the bridge. Some of the famous buildings on this street were Farwell hall, McVicker's theatre, the Morrison block, *Tribune* building, *Staats Zeitung* building, and St. Mary's church. The entire street was built up with blocks such as cannot be excelled in any city.

Monroe street, from river to lake, having upon it the Lombard block, the postoffice, the *Prairie Farmer* building, and a large number of the finest blocks in the city; Adams street, with its cheaper buildings at the west end, its Academy of Design, with most of the works of art therein contained, its temple of Swedenborg, the south side reservoir, and many other buildings; Quincy street, with its Pacific hotel, fast approaching completion, and its Palmer house, the pride of everybody, with its palaces and its dens of infamy and shame; Jackson street, from the residences of the rich and the elegant Trinity church on the east, to the less pretentious houses of the working class farther west, to the hundreds of dens and holes of darkness at the west, were illuminated and oxygenized.

Van Buren street, with its bridge, its magnificent railway depot, St. Paul's church, the Academy of Science building, and its blocks of fine residences and acres of poor ones, were annihilated.

Congress street, with its elegant Second Congregational church; Harrison street, with its freight-house, the Jones school building, and every thing else, except the Methodist church on Wabash avenue, and

NEW YORK

UNDERWRITERS AGENCY

Cash Assets,

THREE MILLION DOLLARS.

....*Agent.*

www.ingramcontent.com/pod-product-compliance
Lightning Source LLC
LaVergne TN
LVHW011132110826
845150LV00008B/2302
* 9 7 8 1 4 1 8 1 9 4 4 6 8 *